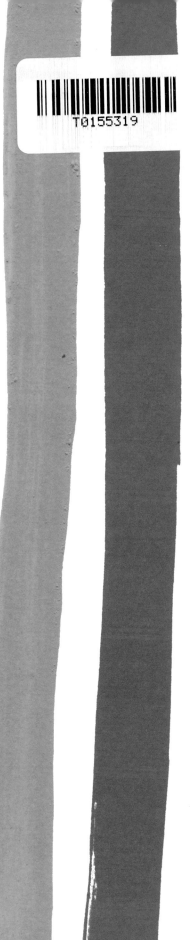

To my parents, who helped me grow.
—S.A.S.

For Marthe, for all. With thanks to Marianna.
—T.S.

Text copyright © 2011 by Susan A. Shea

Illustrations copyright © 2011 by Tom Slaughter

All rights reserved / CIP Data is available.

Published in the United States 2011 by

🍎 Blue Apple Books

South Orange, New Jersey

www.blueapplebooks.com

10/17   Printed in China

ISBN: 978-1-60905-062-7

1 0   9

# DO YOU KNOW WHICH ONES WILL GROW?

Susan A. Shea

paintings by **Tom Slaughter**

🍎 Blue Apple Books

If you look around
you'll see,
Some things grow,
like you and me.

Others stay the way
they're made,
Until they crack, or rust,
or fade.

Fresh

Do you know which ones will grow?

Think, then answer

**YES** or

**NO.**

If a **duckling** grows

and becomes a **duck**,

can a **car** grow

and become . . .

a **truck**?

If a **cub** grows
and becomes a **bear**,

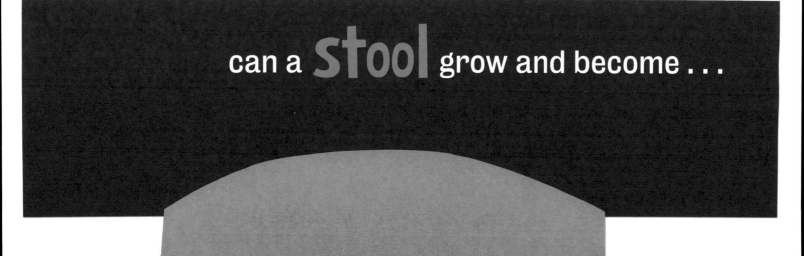

can a **stool** grow and become . . .

Aa Bb Cc Dd

Ll Mm Nn Oo

a chair?

If a **kitten** grows

and becomes a **cat,**

can a **cap** grow and become . . .

a **hat**?

If a **kid** grows

and becomes a **goat**,

can a **sweater** grow

and become . . .

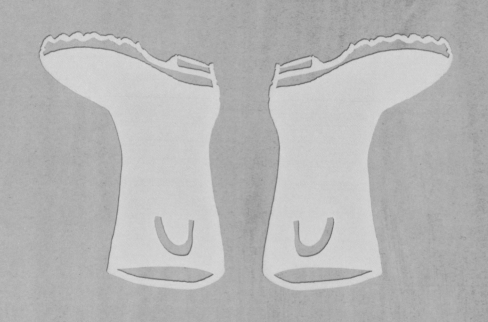

a coat?

If an **owlet** grows and becomes an **owl**,

can a **washcloth** grow and become . . .

a towel?

**YES** to ducks, bears, and owls.

**NO** to trucks, chairs, and towels.

Fresh

**YES** to cats.

**YES** to goats.

**NO** to hats.

**NO** to coats.

If a **calf** grows and becomes a **cow**,

can a
**shovel**
grow and become . . .

a plow?

If a **snakelet** grows

and becomes a **snake**,

can a

**cupcake**

grow and become . . .

a cake?

If a **piglet** grows

and becomes a **pig,**

can a
# pickup truck
grow and become . . .

a **rig?**

If a **kit** grows and becomes a **fox**,

can a

## watch

grow and

become . . .

a clock?

If a **joey** grows

and becomes a **kangaroo**,

can a
**baby**
grow and
become . . .

YOU?

**YES** to cows.

**YES** to snakes.

**NO** to plows.

**NO** to cakes.

**YES** to pigs

**YES** to fox.

**NO** to rigs.

**NO** to clocks.

**YES** to a jumping kangaroo.

**YES** to a living, growing you!